THIS BOOK IS DEDICATED TO OUR PRECIOUS PLANET
FOR WE ARE HER EXTENSIONS AND FOR HER WE SHALL LIVE!

BALAVI
ba•la•vi
/ball-ah-vee/

pronoun
       - A girl who speaks for the planet Earth

adjective
       -(bala) balance (vi) life
              - Living in balance
              - Balance alive

Printed and bound in the United States of America.

ISBN-13: 978-1502420985
ISBN-10: 1502420988

First edition First printing

Graphic design specialist Megan McKearney

Written, illustrated and self published by Mary Chapman
mchap2486@gmail.com

BALAVI

ONCE UPON A TIME,
AS THE SUN SHONE BRIGHT,
WITH ALL OF HER MIGHT,
A SINGLE DROP OF LIGHT BROKE FREE...

It fell down to Earth and from it was a birth
of a girl named Balavi.

She stood in her power
at the top of a flower,
wee as a honey bee.

She comes with a message
and things we must do,
and today is her day
to share them with you.

I am Balavi
I speak for this planet

She has a small wish
and I know we can grant it.

SHE'S CHEERY AND WELL MOST OF THE TIME

BUT DAYS LIKE THESE, SHE ISN'T SO FINE.

BUT WE ARE HER CARETAKERS

AND GET HER WELL

WE WILL!

A CHALLENGE TO YOU, TO SEEK AND TO CHERISH,
A RELATIONSHIP WITH OUR PLANET
THAT WILL NOT LET HER PERISH.

BECAUSE I KNOW WE CAN
NURTURE AND CARE,
RESPECT AND SHINE LIGHT
ON ALL LIFE OUT THERE.

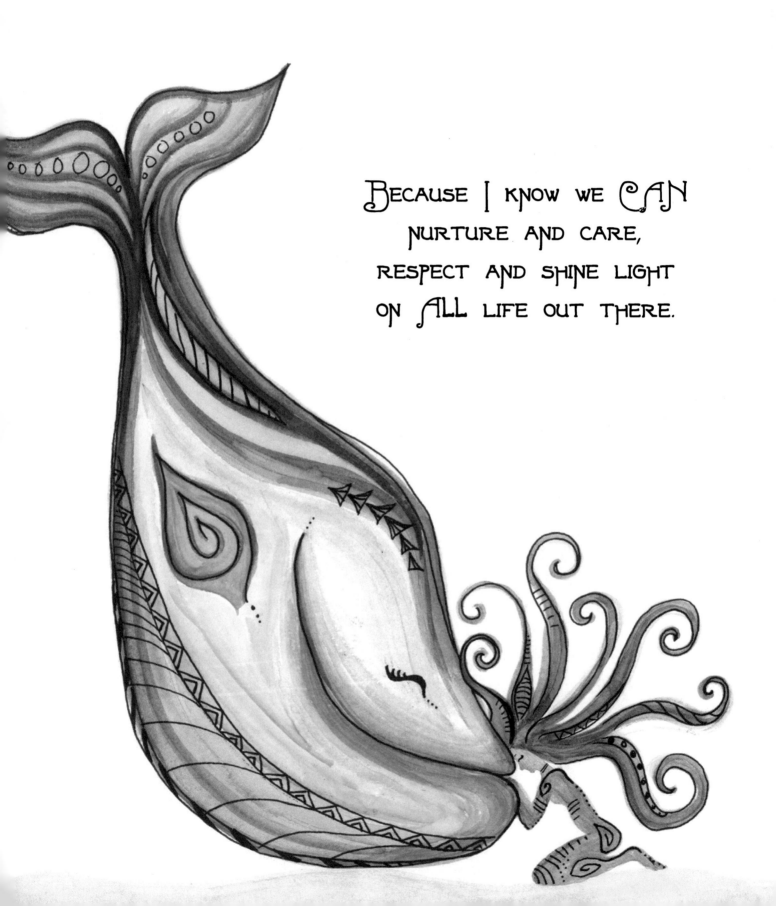

Air
NEEDS OUR HELP
TO BREATHE
DEEPER TOGETHER

So ALL CREATURES THAT NEED TO
CAN DO SO FOREVER

WE MUST FILL OURSELVES UP
WITH THE GOOD AIR THERE IS
AND SEEK OUT A LIFE
WHERE THE WINGED ONES
CAN LIVE.

IMAGINE MAGICAL CLOUDS
WITH NO SMOG OR POLLUTION

AND BIRDS

WHO CAN FLIT

WITHOUT OUR INTRUSION.

A PLACE WHERE AIR
WILL CLEANSE
YOUR SOUL,

A HEALTHY BREEZE
FOR TUMBLE WEEDS
TO ROLL.

FOR WE SHARE OUR BREATH
WITH THE BEES AND THE TREES,
FROM GREEN LUNG TO RED LUNG
GOOD OXYGEN WE ALL NEED.

A WISE ONE ONCE SAID...

"THE MORE FRESH AIR YOU INSPIRE,
        THE GREATER YOU'LL FEEL
            WHEN IT'S TIME TO RETIRE!"

WE HONOR THE SECURITY

OF THE INVISIBLE PURITY

THE LIFE-GIVING FORCE

IN EVERY CELL

THE BREATH BEHIND

EACH STORY WE TELL

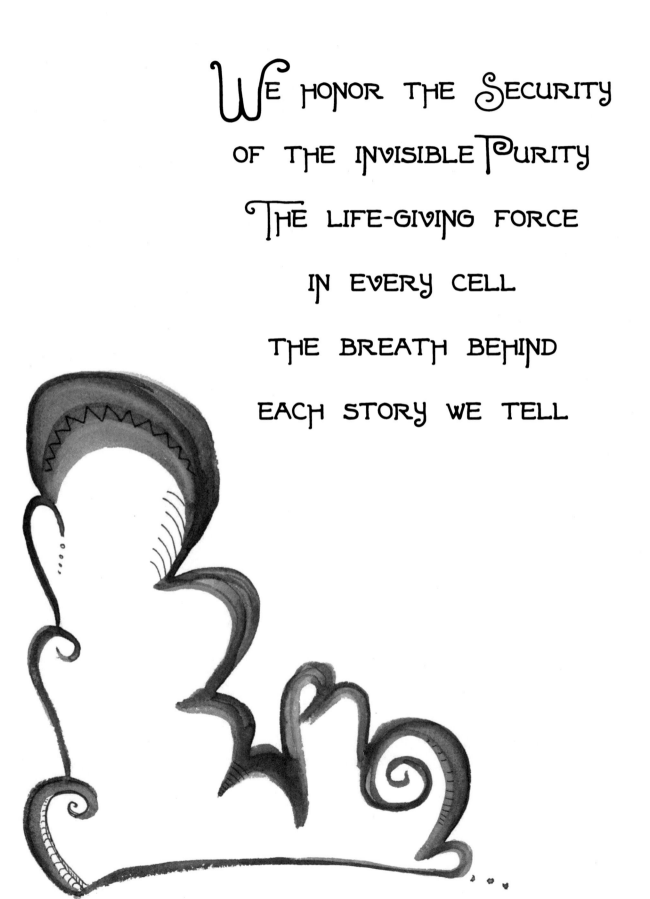

Sizzle POP!
Flicker FLAME
Passion ignited
this is no game

STOKE HER
AND FEEL HER
WITH CARE AND GRACE.
LET HER WARM YOUR CHILLY FACE.

THE BREATH OF PELE
~ HAAAAAAA ~

THE BIRTH OF LAND...

THE GREAT FIRE SPIRIT
AND HER BURNING HOT BAND...

BRINGS CLEANSING TO PLACES WHERE BALANCE IS NEEDED
SPARKING UP NEW LIFE WHERE THE OLD IS DEPLETED

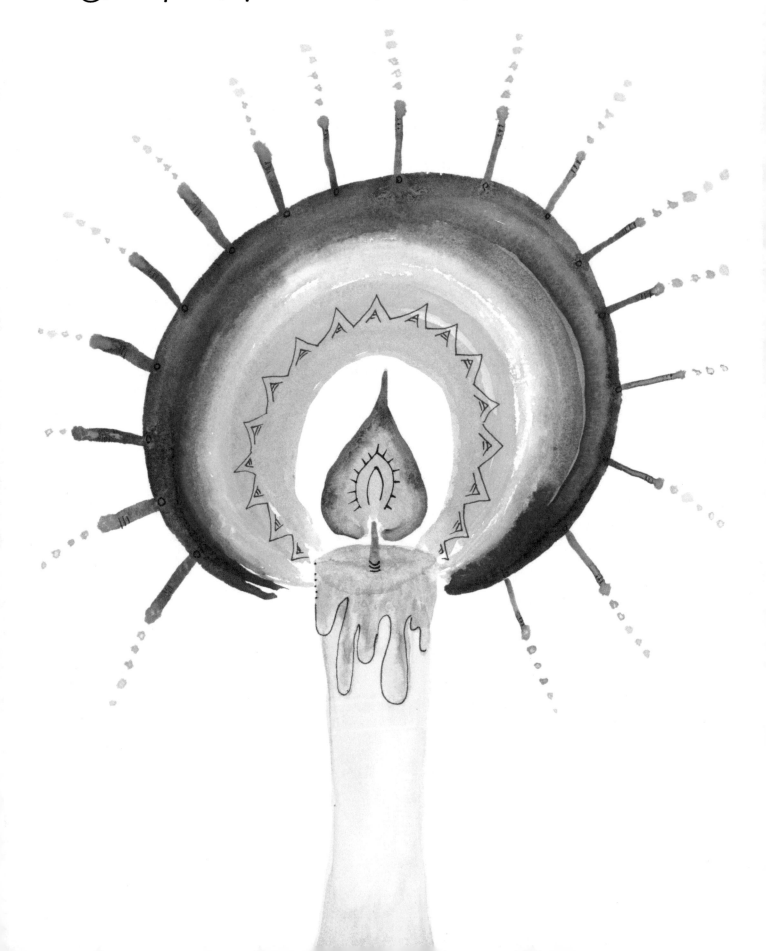

WE HONOR YOUR POWER
TO PUT UP A GREAT FIGHT
TO TAKE WHAT IS WRONG
AND BURN IT TO RIGHT

WISH I MAY, WISH I MIGHT
BECOME AS FIERCE
AS YOUR FLAMES TONIGHT

AND GROW WITH ANGST
AND NEVER HOLD BACK
THE SOURCE IS CALLING
OUR TENDER ATTACK

TO LOVE AND BE LOVED
TO OUR GREATEST POTENTIAL
AND SHINE ON OTHERS
AND HOLD THEM SO GENTLE

Because like our sun, we hold a great light

And like brother fire, we can spread it out...right?!

FROM THE DEPTHS OF THE OCEAN WRITHING WITH LIFE

CREATURES EMERGE, JELLY AND TENTACLE-LIKE

FED BY THE CYCLE
PERFECT WITHOUT
HUMAN HELP

FROM SUNSHINE TO PLANKTON, TO GIANT SEA KELP

For great reef sharks and magical whales
Life is celebrated
in joyful flicks
of tails

Interfere we must NOT
Rather respect them a lot

For they are the keepers of this mysterious bubble
A liquid embrace deserves none of our trouble

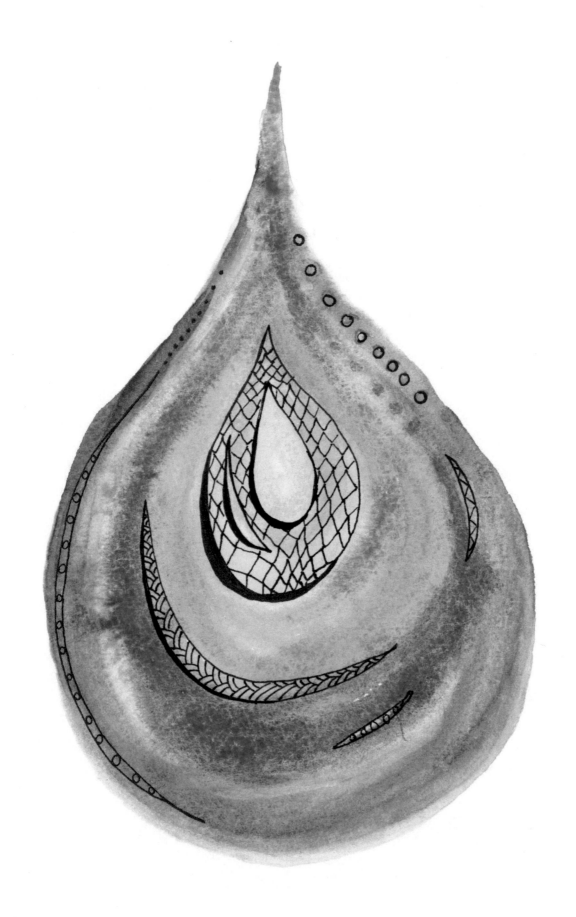

WE HONOR THE POWER IN YOUR GREAT MIGHTY WAVES
AND RESPECT THAT WE NEED YOU THROUGHOUT ALL OUR DAYS

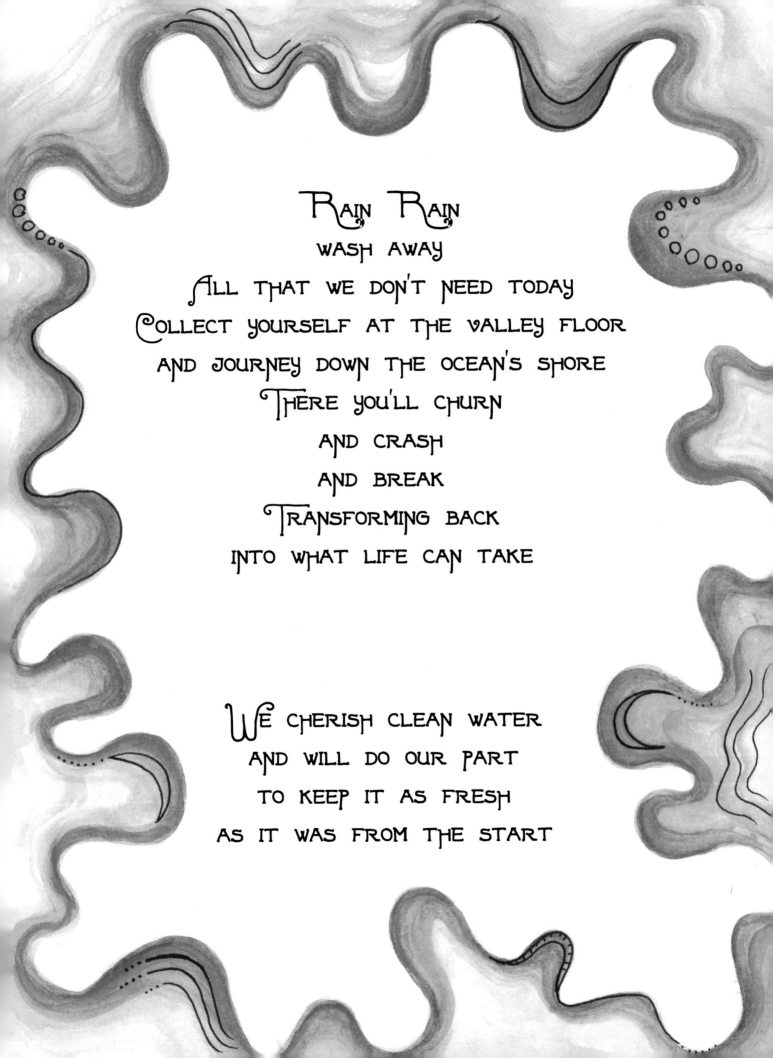

Rain Rain
wash away
All that we don't need today
Collect yourself at the valley floor
And journey down the ocean's shore
There you'll churn
and crash
and break
Transforming back
into what life can take

We cherish clean water
and will do our part
to keep it as fresh
as it was from the start

GROUNDED GAIA, GRANDMOTHER EARTH

I FEEL YOU, I SURRENDER

TO YOUR SOLID ROUND GIRTH

Bleeding and weeping
your trees
are in danger

But we can listen to her needs
as more than a stranger

She speaks through her mosses
her flower and soil

Her life is Our life
as a friend, she is MOST loyal

So STAND **TALL** AND REPRESENT THE HEALTH THAT SHE IS

FOR WE ARE HER EXTENSIONS

AND FOR HER WE SHALL LIVE!

A TOAST
TO THE SEASONS
FOR GROWTH BEYOND REASONS
A TASK AT HAND
WHICH OUR SURVIVAL DOES COMMAND

In a joyous way
and wearing a
smile

Can we please
just be still
for awhile?

To ask the flames
and the breeze
and the trees...

To call out to the depths
of the GIANT blue seas...

What is it You Feel?
How can we Help You Heal?

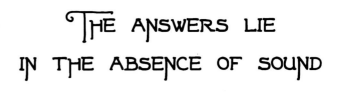

THE ANSWERS LIE
IN THE ABSENCE OF SOUND

IN THE FLAP OF THE WING

OR THE HUM IN THE GROUND...

Be the messenger
be the voice

And know that you
really do have a choice

You can turn away
and pretend it's all right

Or you can share your gifts
and spread your light!

You See...

Balavi

Is not just a name for ME

Finding balance in life

is a task for ALL of humanity

We do need every one of you
To be real, be ready
be honest and true

Loving yourself through all that you do

Because you can't love your planet
if you can't love You

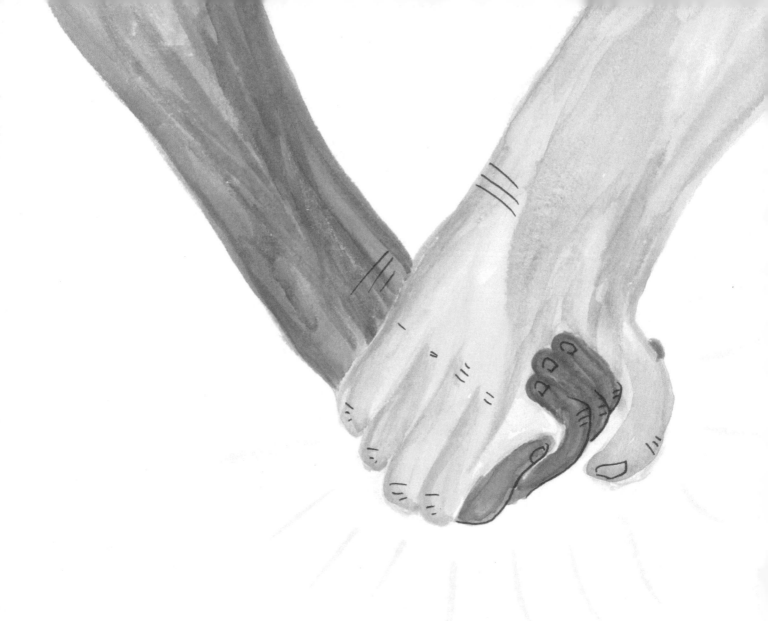

So commit to loving yourself
through and through
Because when we do
whether we meant to or not
We shine brighter together
and light up the whole lot

THE BRIGHTER WE SHINE
AND THE MORE LOVE THAT WE SHARE

THE HURT AND THE PAIN AND THE YUCK
WE REPAIR!

The End